Beautiful Baby Faces

A book celebrating emotions and diversity

"Every child is a different kind of flower, and all together, make this world a beautiful garden."
– Author Unknown

Happy

Can you find
the baby that is
happy?

Surprised

Can you find
the baby that is
surprised?

Afraid

Can you find
the baby that is
afraid?

Angry

Can you find the baby that is angry?

Disgusted

Can you find
the baby that is
disgusted?

Sad

Can you find the baby that is sad?

Curious

Can you find
the baby that is
curious?

Sleeping

Can you find
the baby that is
sleeping?

Printed in Poland
by Amazon Fulfillment
Poland Sp. z o.o., Wrocław